MYSTERIES
OF THE ANCIENT WORLD

THE HOLY GRAIL
CHRISTOPHER KNIGHT
AND ROBERT LOMAS

WEIDENFELD & NICOLSON
LONDON

L egends come and go but the story of the Holy Grail has endured in western folklore ever since the middle of the 12th century. Today the phrase 'seeking the Holy Grail' means any

*G*lastonbury Tor, where Joseph of
Arimathea was reputed to have planted
his staff as the Holy Thorn tree.

search for definitive knowledge, and has a connotation of something as illusory and futile as hunting for the pot of gold at the end of a rainbow.

The Power of the Holy Grail

The most common definition of the Holy Grail is that it was the sacred cup from which Jesus Christ drank at the Last Supper. According to common legend this precious cup was kept by a man who gave up his own tomb so that Jesus could be buried in a way befitting the Messiah. This man was Joseph of Arimathea, who is said to have used the holy cup to collect the blood that flowed from Christ's wounds as he was nailed to the cross. Many years later Joseph left Jerusalem with the Grail to travel to Glastonbury in Britain where he arrived in AD 73. From that time onwards, it is said, the Grail has been secretly transmitted from generation to generation of Joseph's descendants in the British Isles.

There have also been other variations of the legend of the Holy Grail which describe it not as any kind of cup, but as the 'the stone upon which kings are made' or even as 'a book that contains the secret teachings of Jesus'.

Most people today assume that the Holy Grail is purely mythical, and yet many serious-minded researchers have found cause to investigate the possibility of it being a real artefact. Until relatively recently we would have sided fully with the sceptics, considering it no more than a medieval Christian myth. But two years ago, whilst researching something quite different we stumbled upon new evidence that changed our view completely.

One does not have to believe in magic or miracles to have an interest in the Holy Grail because there is real history as well as myth to consider. It is widely accepted that Jesus Christ was once a living person and, as he has been hailed as the Son of God from his own time to this,

The Holy Grail as depicted in German legend.

*K*ing Arthur
    shown in
a 12th-century
mosaic.

it is not unreasonable to assume that his followers could have preserved this ceremonial drinking cup. Had they done so it would certainly have been venerated and viewed as the greatest treasure in the whole of Christendom.

If the Holy Grail was preserved after the crucifixion of Jesus it must have been kept very secret for the first 1,100 hundred years, because the very first written reference did not appear until around 1140. The story of the Holy

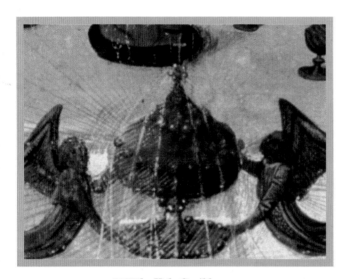

The Holy Grail borne aloft by angels.

Grail was quickly connected to the mythical story of King Arthur, which had been introduced just a few years earlier.

The popular versions of the Arthurian legend and the Grail that we all see in films and on television today are mainly based on the later romantic works of Sir Thomas Mallory, written in the 15th century. In these tales the Grail is said to possess many miraculous properties, such as the power of furnishing food for those without sin, of blinding the impure of heart or striking dumb the irreverent who come into its presence.

Great legends develop and are sustained because they hold values that people admire and the delicate line between fact and fiction often becomes blurred. With most of these folk tales it is impossible to identify where and when they started, but the story of the Grail is unusual because it has a definite

The Grail Temple as depicted in Neuschwanstein Castle.

*A*rthur and
*his knights
seated at their
famous round
table. From a
15th-century
French painting.*

*M*almesbury Abbey, where William first wrote the story of Joseph of Arimathea and the Grail.

*A*rthur as portrayed by Robert de Boron in 1199.

starting point. The first the world knew of such an artefact was from the pen of an ageing monk and historian who lived in Malmesbury Abbey, between Oxford and Bristol. William of Malmesbury composed his saga of Joseph of Arimathea shortly after a nearby cleric called Geoffrey of Monmouth had published the first story of King Arthur in his book *The Matter of Britain*.

The two ecclesiastical neighbours both claimed to know the truth and each accused each the other of telling false accounts of King Arthur. From the very first references the Holy Grail was described as having been lost at some earlier date, and the task for all concerned was to recover the missing treasure.

Geoffrey of Monmouth claimed that his story was historically accurate and that he had found the details recorded in an old document that had been brought to his attention. His story depicted King Arthur as a supernatural

C raig y Ddinas,
 in Wales, one
of the many sites
claimed as the place
where Arthur still
sleeps.

G awain, from the French 15th-century work entitled Romance of the Grail.

THE
HOLY
GRAIL

saviour of his people with a kingdom at Caerleon, beginning in the year AD 505 and ending when the King was carried westwards to the sacred isle of Avalon, where he rests until a time of great need when he will return again.

When these stories first appeared they quickly spread across the whole of Europe and for several centuries were considered to be historical fact.

Just at the time that these fabulous stories were becoming popular a new order of knights was making a name for itself and many people considered them to be as magical and inspiring as the Knights of the Round Table. The Knights Templar were a strange order of crusader monks based in

he knights of the Round Table with the Grail, from a 14th-century French drawing.

mort en faient remambrance les hons qui apres
uenront. et ace sacordent tous. si entrerent en laca
prindrent les armes de telr en y eut pour iouster
assur. et de telr en y eut qui ne prindreut fors que
couuertures et leurs escus. Car mout se fioient
prouesses leurs plusieurs. Et le roy qui tout ce ot
ne lauoit fait fors pour ueoir une partie dela che
leue galaad. Car bien pensoit quil ne reuiendroit
mais ...

Jerusalem, who were said to have found the Holy Grail and to have become its secret guardians. The Templars adopted white tunics with a large red cross and they grew shoulder-length hair and beards in the style of 1st-century priests of Jerusalem. Their dress has now become synonymous with the image of a crusader.

Within months of their establishment in 1128 they became fabulously rich and rumours spread that they conducted strange initiation ceremonies in secret.

The Treasures of Jerusalem

To understand how the Knights Templar could have been connected with a relic that they believed was the Holy Grail we must now return to 1st-century Jerusalem to find the possible root of the legend of the Holy Grail.

As we, and other researchers have found, the stories told in the New Testament are not a very accurate rendering of events. Many leading churchmen will now admit that many of the stories told in the Gospels are largely myth, conveying the spirit of Christianity rather than its history. The Jerusalem Church believed that there was a need for two messiahs; one to be king and one to be high priest. These messiahs were not viewed as gods but as earthly leaders who would create a kingdom fit for their God, Yahweh, to rule over. At the very centre of the Jewish faith was the Temple at Jerusalem, built by Solomon and rebuilt by King Herod during the lifetime of Jesus and his brother James.

At the eastern entrance of the Jerusalem Temple stood two pillars called Boaz and Jachin, which were believed to represent the power of the two messiahs – one of a kingly line, descended from David, and one of a priestly line, descended from Aaron, the priestly brother of Moses.

*T**he kingly pillar of Boaz which stood outside Solomon's Temple, reproduced in Roslin Chapel by William St Clair in the mid-15th century.*

The city of Jerusalem viewed from the east. The Dome of the Rock was built by Muslims in the 7th century upon the ruins of Herod's temple.

After Jesus was crucified he was succeeded by his brother James, who was himself murdered in AD 62. Possibly because of the killing of James, the Jews started a terrible war that eventually led to the destruction of them and their Temple.

The strange truth is that by the time the authors of the Gospels of Matthew, Mark, Luke and John first put pen to paper everyone who had known Jesus and his followers was dead, along with most of the population of Israel. Although the Bible does not mention it, we know from a man called Josephus, who was an eye-witness to the destruction of Jerusalem, that over 1.3 million Jewish men women and children died by the sword between AD 66 and 73.

The most devout Jews, including the group we now call the Jerusalem Church, had acquired the great wealth of the city and it is now known that they believed that they were instructed by

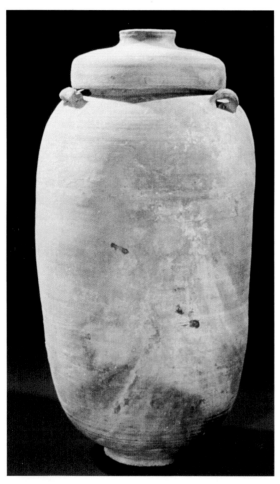

*O*ne of the jars which contained the Dead Sea Scrolls found in Qumran in 1947.

God to bury their most precious artefacts beneath the Temple in Jerusalem, as close as they could get to the 'Holy of Holies' – the inner chamber where God Himself was present.

In 1946 a cache of scrolls was found hidden in a desert location south-east of Jerusalem, which had been the site of the religious Jewish community of Qumran 2,000 years ago. Among these famous documents, known to us as the Dead Sea Scrolls, was a very important list, written on copper, which records how the Jews buried their treasure underneath the Temple before the Romans made their final assault. This Copper Scroll identifies exactly where different treasures and scrolls were buried and it lists bars of gold, hundreds of pitchers of silver coins, scrolls and many cups and other vessels; fabulous riches by any standards.

This Copper Scroll was written just before the fall of the Temple and the twelfth entry, typical of the 61 entries, says:

In the Court of [unreadable word], nine cubits under the southern corner: gold and silver vessels for tithe, sprinkling basins, cups, sacrificial bowls, libation vessels, in all six hundred and nine.

These artefacts were buried by a group which included many people who had known Jesus personally. If a cup or sacrificial blood-collecting bowl associated with Jesus existed, it would have been buried here with the treasures of the Jews.

These Jewish resistance fighters buried their precious objects in the spring of AD 68, and the Dead Sea Scrolls were hidden in the caves around Qumran shortly afterwards. They acted just in time, because Roman forces destroyed Qumran only weeks later, in the month of June. Two years later the holy Temple of the Jews lay in ruins and the members of the Jerusalem Church had been slain by the Romans. All memory of the secret horde was lost. The Holy Grail and everything precious to the people that knew Jesus Christ was buried under thousands of tons of tumbled masonry.

*T*he cave at Qumran where the Copper Scroll was found. It describes the treasure the Knights Templar excavated from Jerusalem.

The Kings of God

The priests of the Temple of Jerusalem preserved the genealogies of the lines of David and Aaron and the Bible tells us that Jesus was descended from David on Joseph's side and from Aaron on Mary's side, making him a possible messiah for both lines. Our own recent research has indicated that when the Romans destroyed the Temple in AD 70, some of the hereditary priests of the Temple managed to escape to Europe in order to preserve their 1,000-year-old bloodlines.

It is very interesting to note that legend says that Joseph of Arimathea brought the Holy Grail to Britain in AD 73; just three years after the fall of the Temple. This is significant because the originators of the Grail stories were

J oseph of Arimathea bringing the Holy Grail and the Holy Thorn tree to Glastonbury, and, right, as shown in a 15th-century English painting.

*J*osephus, son of Joseph of Arimathea, shown with the Grail; from the 14th-century French **Queste de Saint-Graal.**

Christians and it is unlikely that they would have realized the importance of this date because the New Testament does not record the fall of the Jerusalem Temple.

While the date fits well, there is a problem with the idea that Joseph of Arimathea travelled to Britain in AD 73 and then continued his bloodline. The difficulty is that we are told in the Bible that Joseph allowed Jesus to be buried in the tomb that had prepared for himself. Jesus had died around 40 years before, so Joseph must have been a very young man at the time of the Crucifixion; and young men do not usually spend money preparing their own graves.

It seems probable that the people who arrived in Britain were the children or even grandchildren of Joseph of Arimathea and it is his bloodline that was important. We also have good reason to believe that these descendants of the hereditary priests of the Temple did not have the Holy Grail with them. It was already lost . . . but they knew where it rested – under the ruins of Herod's Temple.

Over the following centuries the descendants of the surviving high priests of the Temple founded some of the leading families of Europe and they secretly transmitted the story of the lost Holy Grail down the generations for the next 1,000 years.

By the end of the 11th century these families were fully Christianized on the surface, but secretly they knew the location of the Holy Grail and all of the great treasures of their Jewish ancestors. These families with ancient Jewish bloodlines called themselves 'Rex Deus', which is Latin for 'the kings of God' – but only a chosen son of each generation was told the full secrets of their past and the story of the treasures buried under the Temple.

G odfrey de Bouillon taking Jerusalem in 1099.

These families included the Counts of Champagne, the Counts of Anjou, the St Clairs, the Counts of Fountain and the de Bouillon family, and in 1071 something happened that caused these families to return to Jerusalem.

That year the city was devastated by Seljuk Turks which the Rex Deus families saw as the fulfilment of a prophecy written in the Book of Revelations that said Jerusalem would be attacked by heathens led by Gog and Magog, 1,000 years after the fall of the city in AD 70. In chapter 20 the visionary author describes how the resurrected martyrs who had died defending Jerusalem from the Romans, would return at this time.

The Turks had taken the city exactly 1,000 years later and the Rex Deus families saw themselves as the 'resurrected' bloodline who would return to free

Hugues de Payens being invested as the first Grand Master of the Knights Templar by Pope Honorius.

Jerusalem. They used their considerable influence to raise the greatest army that Europe had ever seen, and on 15 July 1099 these crusaders captured Jerusalem. Then, with an efficiency not seen since Roman times, they massacred every man, woman and child in the name of God.

The Rex Deus families then turned their attention to establishing the strange order of the Knights Templar who were both priests and warriors. They knew of the treasures that lay beneath the ruins of the Temple of Jerusalem from the stories that had been handed down from father to son for 1,000 years, and in 1118 they started excavating below the ruined Temple.

Amongst the wonderful treasures that they found was a particularly precious vessel, and whilst many items must have been melted down, this special cup was kept and revered as the Holy Grail itself.

Hugues de Payen, the first Grand Master of the Templars visited Scotland, where his old friend and uncle by marriage, Henri St Clair lived. Henri had been one of the Rex Deus members who captured Jerusalem and on his return to Scotland he had been made a baron. He must have been very excited that the Rex Deus families had used their ancient knowledge to retake Jerusalem exactly as prophesied, and he celebrated the occasion by taking a very unusual title for himself. He called himself the 'Baron of Roslin'. In Scottish Gaelic the short word Roslin has the very significant meaning, 'ancient knowledge passed down the generations'. In 1140 the Templars moved the scrolls and treasures, including the Holy Grail, to lands owned by the St Clair family in Kilwinning, where they built an abbey.

It can be no coincidence that the stories of the Holy Grail and King Arthur suddenly appeared in the 12 years between the finding of the treasures below the Temple and their arrival in Kilwinning. Both of the early creators of the Arthurian and Grail stories had direct contact with Payen de Montdidier, one of the founding Knights Templars when he lived in England.

The stories of Arthur, the Grail Quest and the Templars as guardians of the Grail was soon developed by such medieval writers as Chretien de Troyes and Wolfram von Eschenbach, and later by Thomas Mallory.

The Grail Sanctuary at Roslin

The Templars kept their rituals secret for almost 200 years, until on Friday 13 October 1307 they were arrested as heretics and soon destroyed as an order.

The St Clair family still held the scrolls and some of the treasures from Jerusalem. The question is, did they still have the Holy Grail?

We think the answer is yes, because in 1440 Sir William St Clair decided to build a very strange building which survives to this day. It is a small stone building that has been mistakenly identified as a chapel. Every inch both inside and out is carved with strange symbols, but the strangest feature of all is that below

*R*oslin Chapel, *Midlothian, built by Sir William St Clair to house the secrets of the Templars.*

ground the building is an exact replica of the ground-plan of ruins of the Temple at Jerusalem that the knights Templars excavated. To the west is a replica of the ruined west wall of the Temple, which still stands in Jerusalem, but above ground the building is a like a book carved in stone; but a book that is written in a language that is difficult for us to read.

*P*lan of Roslin showing how the Triple Tau
and the Seal of Solomon formed the design
theme of the whole building.

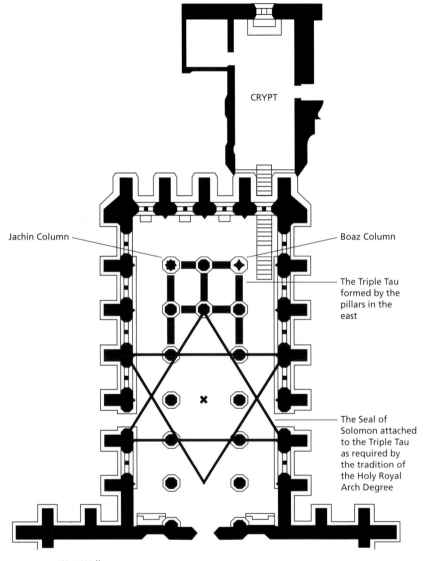

CRYPT

Jachin Column

Boaz Column

The Triple Tau
formed by the
pillars in the
east

The Seal of
Solomon attached
to the Triple Tau
as required by
the tradition of
the Holy Royal
Arch Degree

West Wall

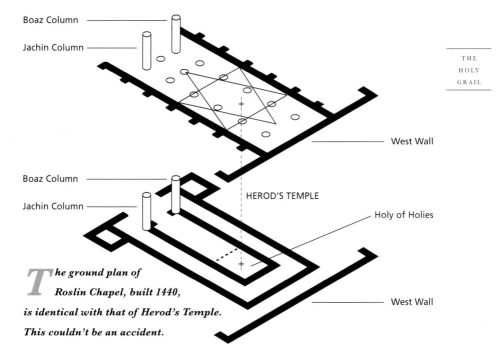

Boaz Column

Jachin Column

West Wall

Boaz Column

Jachin Column

HEROD'S TEMPLE

Holy of Holies

West Wall

*T**he ground plan of Roslin Chapel, built 1440, is identical with that of Herod's Temple. This couldn't be an accident.*

Sir William St Clair of Roslin left clues by adding words to the verbal rituals that had come from the Templars and are still used by Freemasons. In the east are two magnificent pillars, just where they would have been in the Jerusalem Temple, but the other pillars of the building form a symbol called a Triple Tau (referring to the Greek letter of that name). William St Clair tells us through the rituals of Freemasonry that this ancient Jewish symbolic layout has the following mysterious meaning: 'The Temple of Jerusalem, a key to a treasure, a place where a precious thing is concealed, and the precious thing itself.'

This building at Roslin in Scotland has never been excavated so whatever Sir William inherited from the Templars has not been disturbed. What ever ancient knowledge had been passed down the generations he made safe beneath this reconstruction of Herod's Temple and it is almost certain that it is still there. One day soon modern archaeology may be able to once again recover the lost Holy Grail and the secret teachings of Jesus that lie buried with it.

PHOTOGRAPHIC ACKNOWLEDGEMENTS
Cover AKG London/Bibliothèque Nationale,
Paris; pages 2–3 Fortean Picture Library [FPL]/
Paul Broadhurst; pp. 4–5 e.t. archive [ETA];
pp. 6–7 AKG; pp, 8, 9, 10 ETA; p. 12 Zefa;
p. 13 AKG; pp. 14–15 FPL;
pp. 16–17, 18–19 ETA; p. 21 FPL/Andreas
Trottmann; pp. 22–3 Zefa; p. 24 Ancient Art &
Architecture [AAA]; pp. 26–7 AAA; p. 28 FPL;
p. 29 FPL/Roy Fry; pp. 30–31, 32–3 ETA;
pp. 34–5 AKG; p. 37 Bob Lomas.

THE
HOLY
GRAIL

First published in Great Britain 1997
by George Weidenfeld and Nicolson Ltd
The Orion Publishing Group
5 Upper St Martin's Lane
London WC2H 9EA

A CIP catalogue record for this book is available
from the British Library
ISBN 0 297 823183

Picture Research: Suzanne Williams

Design: Harry Green

Typeset in Baskerville